Faces For Feelings

A Workbook:

To improve the ability in all children to recognize feelings expressed on faces
and
a tool for teaching people with Asperger's to recognize how others feel

Happy Mad Scared

Tired Confused Bored

Frustrated Dopey Disgusted

Disappointed Proud Sad

Surprised Curious Shocked

AARON HOORWITZ & ANDREA SHEARER

Copyright © 2022 Aaron Hoorwitz & Andrea Shearer.

All rights reserved. No part of this book may be reproduced, stored, or transmitted by any means—whether auditory, graphic, mechanical, or electronic—without written permission of both publisher and author, except in the case of brief excerpts used in critical articles and reviews. Unauthorized reproduction of any part of this work is illegal and is punishable by law.

ISBN: 979-8-88640-322-0 (sc)
ISBN: 979-8-88640-323-7 (hc)
ISBN: 979-8-88640-324-4 (e)

Because of the dynamic nature of the Internet, any web addresses or links contained in this book may have changed since publication and may no longer be valid. The views expressed in this work are solely those of the author and do not necessarily reflect the views of the publisher, and the publisher hereby disclaims any responsibility for them.

One Galleria Blvd., Suite 1900, Metairie, LA 70001
1-888-421-2397

CONTENTS

Chapter 1 What is the Name of the Feeling on this Face? 1

Chapter 2 What is Different About these Faces? 7

Chapter 3 What is the Same About these Faces? 11

Chapter 4 Do People Always Say What they Really Feel? 18

Chapter 5 What Can You Do After Recognizing a Feeling? 21

Conclusion 26

Acknowledgments 27

About the Authors 28

CHAPTER 1

What is the Name of the Feeling on this Face?

What does she feel?

GLAD   MAD   SAD

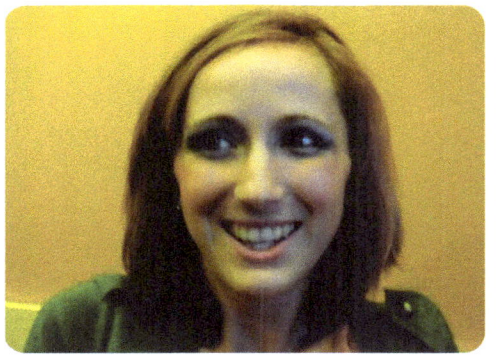

She feels GLAD

Other words for this feeling are:
CHEERFUL   HAPPY   EXCITED

What does she feel?

GLAD   MAD   SAD

She feels MAD

Other words for this feeling are:
ANGRY   ANNOYED   FURIOUS

What does she feel?

GLAD   MAD   SAD

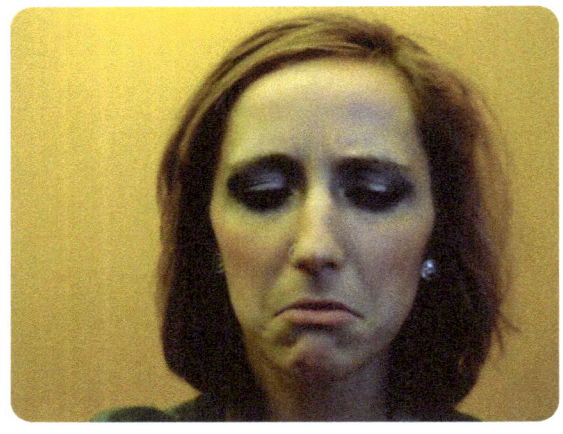

She feels SAD

Other words for this feeling are:
HURT   SORRY   DEPRESSED

What does she feel now?

GLAD   SCARED   TIRED

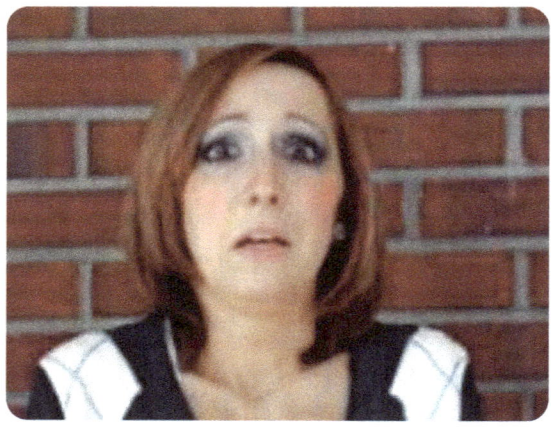

She feels SCARED

Other words for this feeling are:
NERVOUS   AFRAID   TERRIFIED

What does she feel now?

SAD   TIRED   SURPRISED

She feels SURPRISED

Other words for this feeling are:
SHOCKED   STUNNED   AMAZED

What does she feel now?

SAD   TIRED   SURPRISED

She feels TIRED

Other words for this feeling are:
SLEEPY   BORED   EXHAUSTED

What does she feel now?

SCARED   SAD   PROUD

She feels PROUD

Other words for this feeling are:
HAPPY   CONFIDENT   SATISFIED

What does she feel now?

DISGUSTED   HAPPY   PROUD

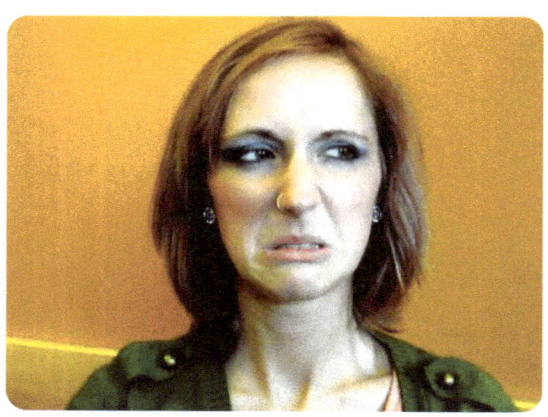

She feels DISGUSTED

Other words for this feeling are:
GROSSED-OUT   NAUSEOUS   HATE

What does she feel now?

HAPPY   CONFUSED   PROUD

She feels CONFUSED

Other words for this feeling are:
UNSURE   CLUELESS   PUZZLED

What does she feel now?

BORED   HAPPY   PROUD

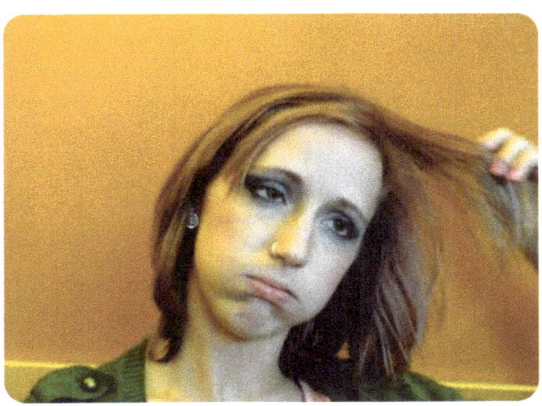

She feels BORED

Other words for this feeling:
TIRED   UNINTERESTED   TURNED-OFF

What does she feel now?

HAPPY   PROUD   DUMB

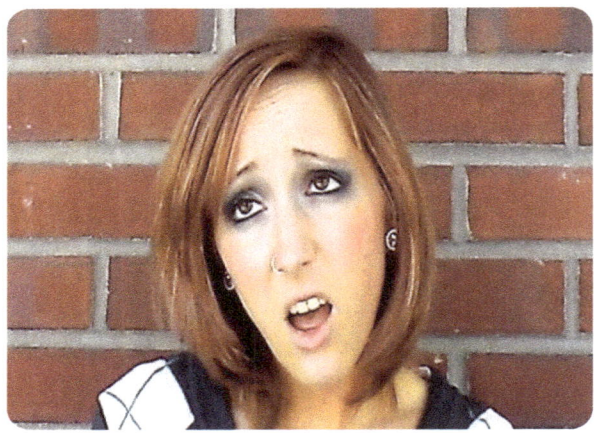

She feels DUMB

Other words for this feeling are:
CLUELESS   STUPID   DOPEY

What does she feel now?

SCARED   HAPPY   SLEEPY

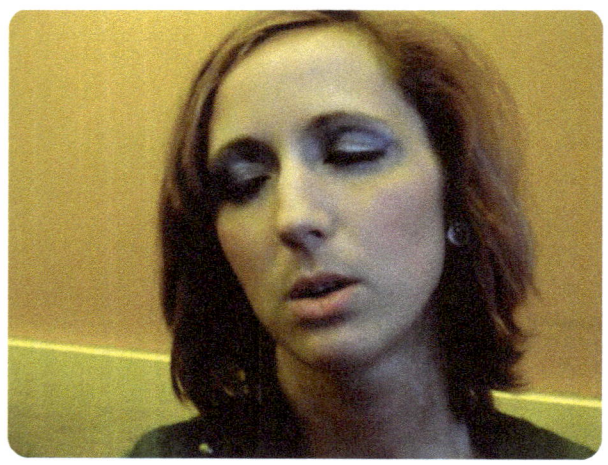

She feels SLEEPY

Other words for this feeling are:
TIRED   EXHAUSTED   WIPED-OUT

CHAPTER 2
What is Different About these Faces?

Which one feels SAD?

  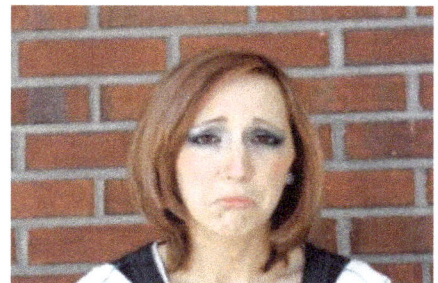

This one feels SAD

Which one feels TIRED?

This one feels TIRED

Which one feels MAD?

This one feels MAD

Which one feels SCARED?

 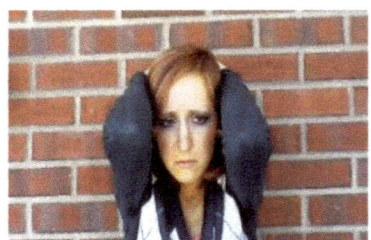 

This one feels SCARED

Which one feels CONFUSED?

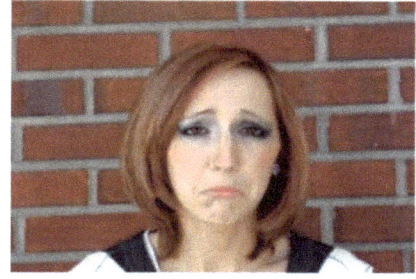  

This one feels CONFUSED

Which one feels PROUD?

 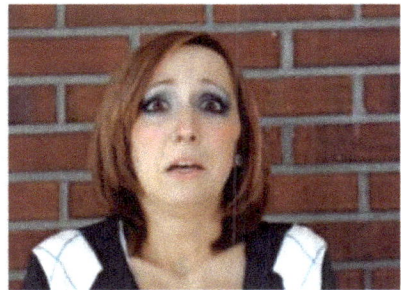 

This one feels PROUD

Which one feels SURPRISED?

This one feels SURPRISED

Which one feels HAPPY?

 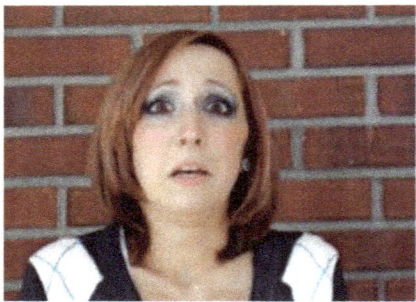 

This one feels HAPPY

CHAPTER 3

What is the Same About these Faces?

Most of these are **SAD** faces.
But one of them doesn't fit because it isn't SAD.
Which one is not SAD?

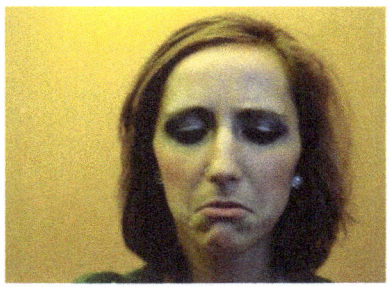

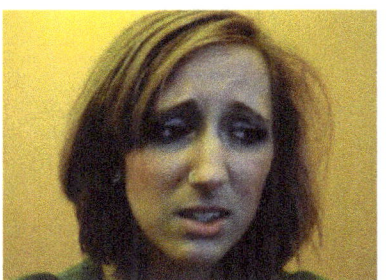

The HAPPY face

Most of these are **HAPPY** faces.
But one of them doesn't fit because it isn't HAPPY.
Which one is not HAPPY?

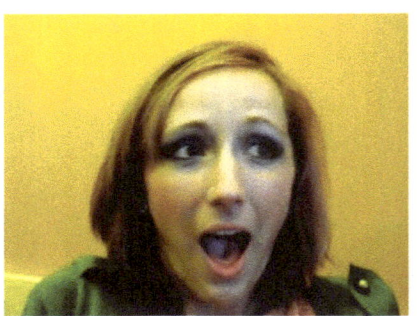
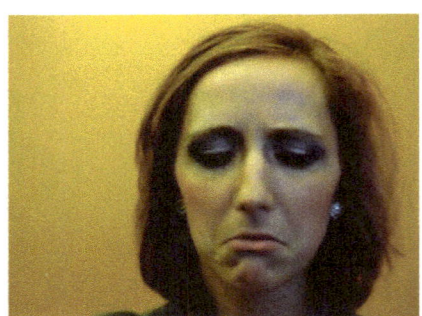
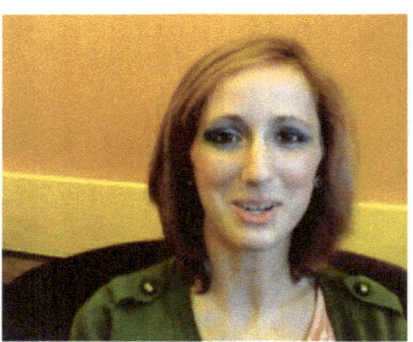
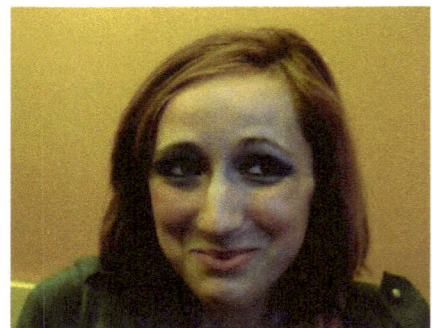

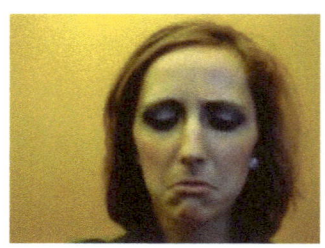

The SAD face

Most of these are **ANGRY** faces.
But one of them doesn't fit because it isn't ANGRY.
Which one is not ANGRY?

The SLEEPY face

Most of these are faces for feeling **CONFUSED**.
But one of them doesn't fit because it isn't CONFUSED.
Which one is not CONFUSED?

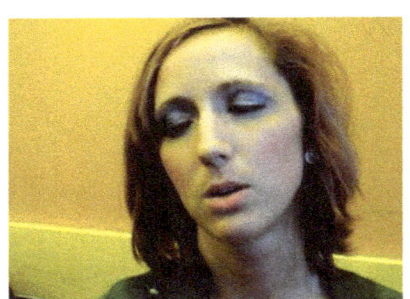

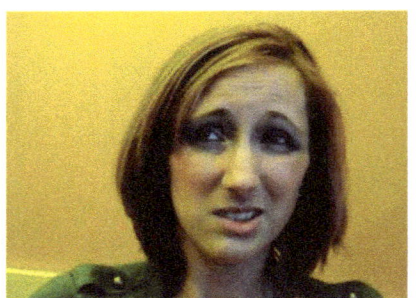

The SLEEPY face

Most of these are faces of feeling **TIRED**.
But one of them doesn't fit because it isn't TIRED.
Which one is not TIRED?

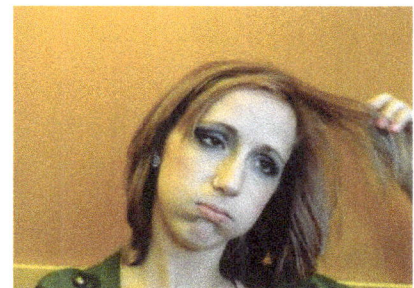
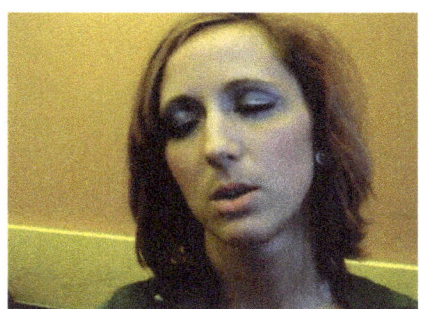

The SCARED face

Most of these are faces of feeling **SCARED**.
But one of them doesn't fit because it isn't SCARED.
Which one is not SCARED?

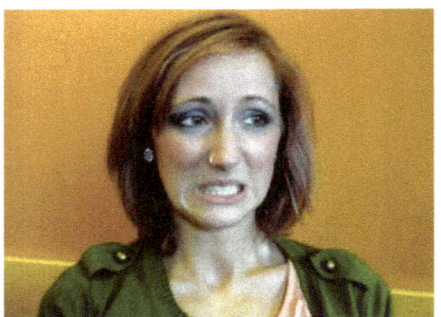

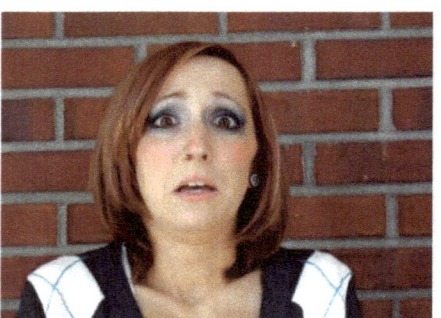

The MAD face

Most of these are faces of feeling **SORRY**.
But one of them doesn't fit because it isn't SORRY.
Which one is not SORRY?

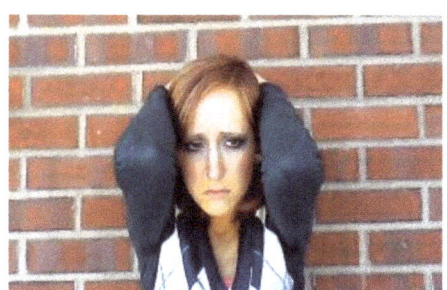 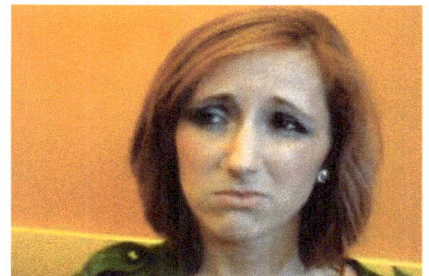

 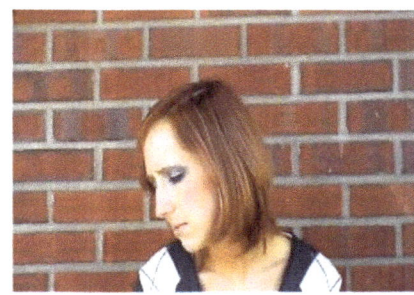

The MAD face

CHAPTER 4
Do People Always Say What they Really Feel?

"You forgot my birthday again? I'm so happy I have such a good boyfriend."

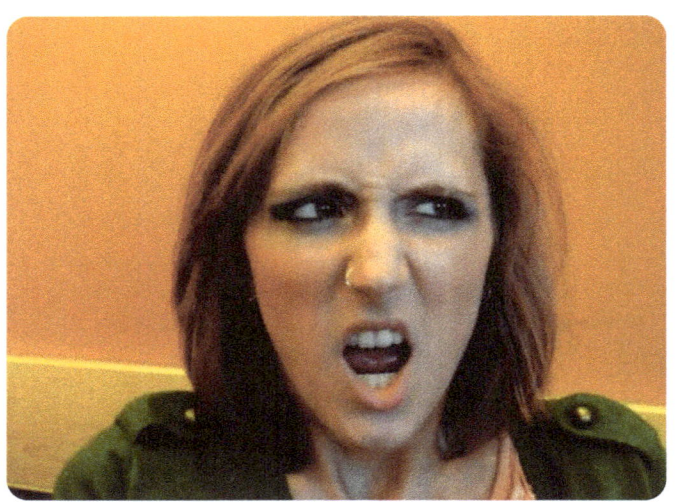

Is she happy like she says she is? Or is she angry?

She's really angry. She doesn't really mean it when she says she's happy with her boyfriend. It's just the way that people talk sometimes.

"Ooh, you scare me when you say you'll tickle me to death."

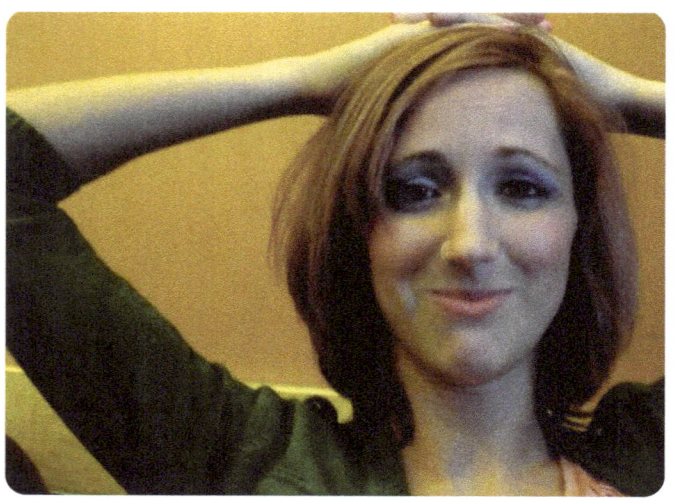

Is she scared like she says she is? Or is she happy and having fun?

She's really happy and having fun. She's just pretending and joking when she says that the tickling scares her. And she doesn't think that she'll die.

"Why do you ask if it makes me happy that we're going to the movies? Can't you see how sad I feel about it?"

Does she feel sad like she said she feels?
Or is she really happy about it?

She's really happy.
She's joking when she says that she's sad about it. It's the way that people talk sometimes.

"Why are you asking if I'm upset about getting yelled at? Can't you see how happy I am about it?"

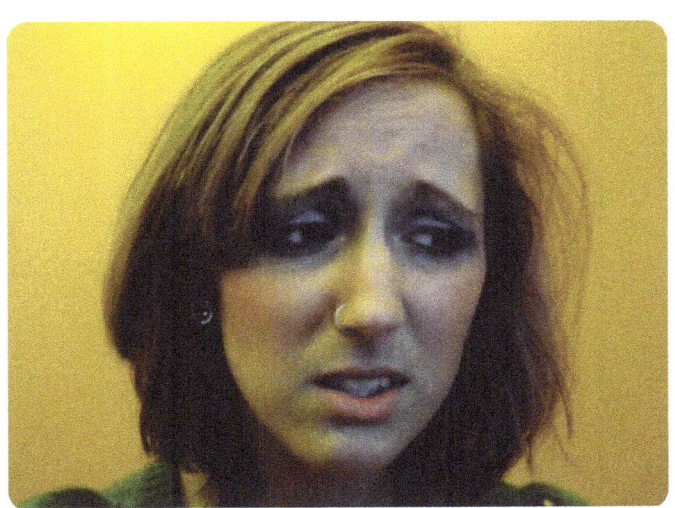

Is she happy like she says she is?
Or is she really upset?

She's really upset.

"What we're having for dinner looks like dog food. Can't you see that I love how it smells? And I can't wait to eat it."

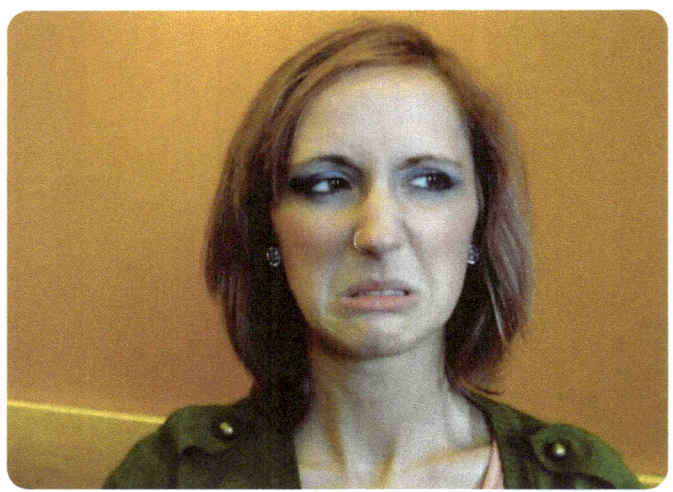

Does she love how it smells?
Does she want to eat it?

Or does she feel disgusted and hate the idea of eating it.

She feels disgusted and doesn't want to eat it.

"Oh, no, I'm not bored at all. Can't you tell that I really want you to keep telling me about this?"

Does she really want him to keep talking? Is she really interested?

Or is she really feeling bored?

She's really feeling so bored that he's putting her to sleep.

CHAPTER 5
What Can You Do After Recognizing a Feeling?

Sometimes you need to say something when someone has a certain feeling.

If you see that someone feels SAD, you can say:
"It looks like you're feeling sad."

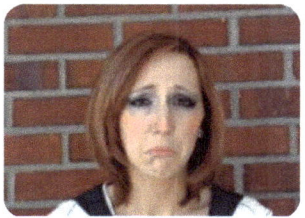

If you see that someone feels HAPPY, you can say:
"It looks like you're feeling happy."

Now you can practice this on the next page.

Look at the picture and say it out loud.

"It looks like you're feeling _____"

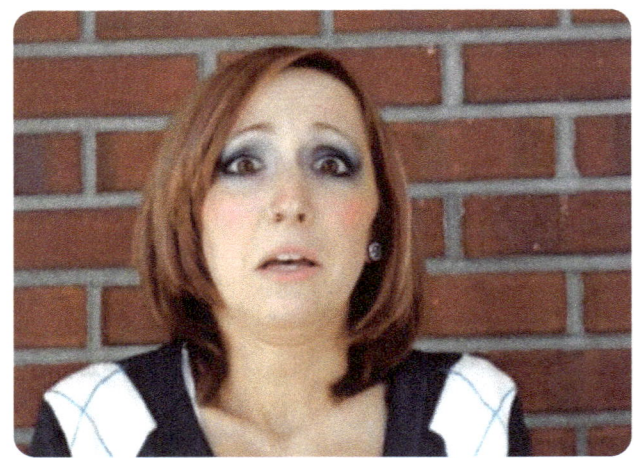

Answers:

"It looks like you're feeling SCARED"

"It looks like you're feeling NERVOUS"

"It looks like you're feeling AFRAID"

"It looks like you're feeling TERRIFIED"

"It looks like you're feeling _____"

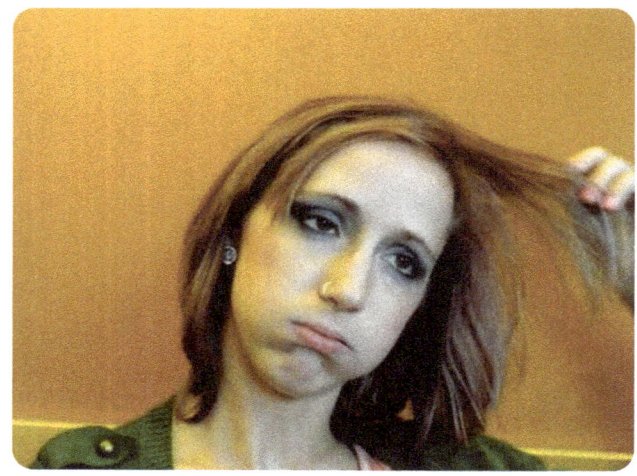

Answers:

"It looks like you're feeling BORED"

"It looks like you're feeling TIRED"

"It looks like you're feeling SLEEPY"

"It looks like you're feeling _____"

Answers:

"It looks like you're feeling MAD"

"It looks like you're feeling ANGRY"

"It looks like you're feeling ANNOYED"

"It looks like you're feeling FURIOUS"

"It looks like you're feeling _____"

Answers:

"It looks like you're feeling CONFUSED"

"It looks like you're feeling UNSURE"

"It looks like you're feeling PUZZLED"

"It looks like you're feeling _____"

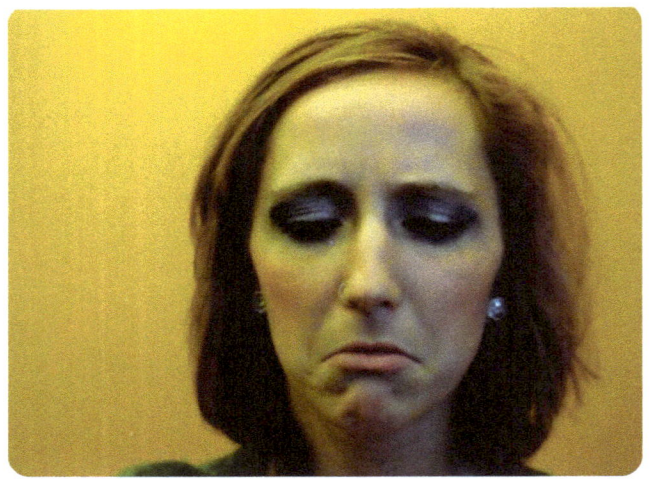

Answers:
"It looks like you're feeling SAD"
"It looks like you're feeling SORRY"
"It looks like you're feeling FRUSTRATED"

"It looks like you're feeling _____"

Answers:
"It looks like you're feeling DISGUSTED"
"It looks like you're feeling GROSSED-OUT"
"It looks like you're feeling SICK"

"It looks like you're feeling _____"

Answers:

"It looks like you're feeling SHOCKED"

"It looks like you're feeling SURPRISED"

"It looks like you're feeling AMAZED"

"It looks like you're feeling _____"

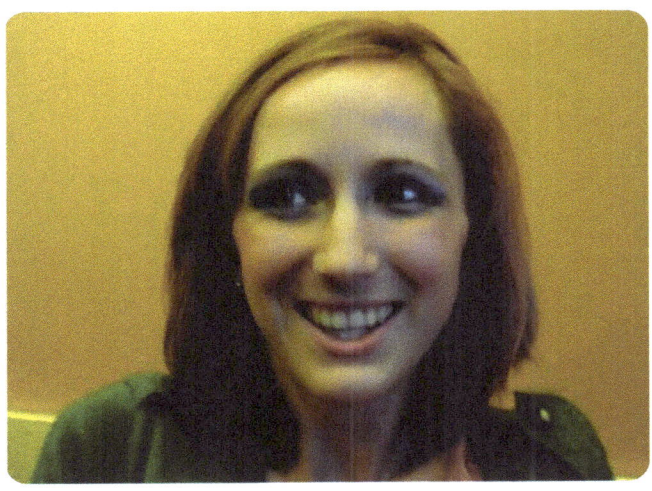

Answers:

"It looks like you're feeling GLAD"

"It looks like you're feeling HAPPY"

"It looks like you're feeling CHEERFUL"

"It looks like you're feeling EXCITED"

CONCLUSION

It can be fun to keep reading this book again and again until you can remember the feeling for each face.

It means that you will be able to know what other people are feeling when you look at their faces.

If you've already started to remember some of the feelings for some of the faces, then maybe your own face will show a certain feeling.

Maybe it will show that you feel PROUD of yourself for doing a good job.

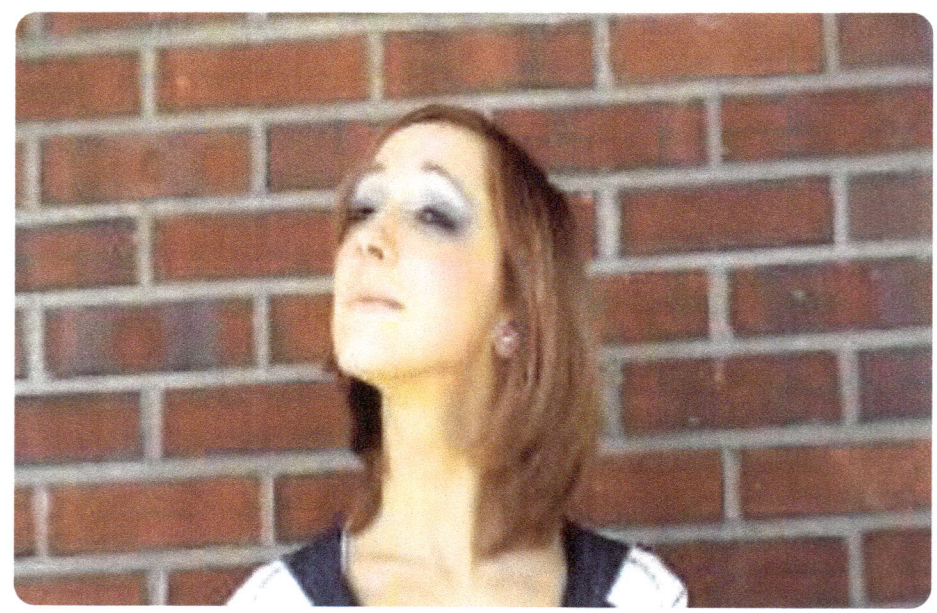

ACKNOWLEDGMENTS

An acknowledgement is given here to Jennifer Smith, who suggested a book of this kind while brainstorming about improving the ability to recognize feelings from expressions on people's faces.

ABOUT THE AUTHORS

Aaron Noah Hoorwitz is a Ph.D. psychologist in private practice in Albany, N.Y., He has taught psychology in local colleges, has published in the professional literature, and worked for many years with the courts and with children as the Chief Psychologist in the Rensselaer County Mental Health Department. His purpose for developing this current book was that he wanted this kind of material to be available to help any child to improve in the ability to recognize people's feelings, including anyone who has difficulty with this ability. A short article he wrote on Asperger's Disorder can be accessed on the internet:*When autism disorders can look like defiance and what to do about it.* https://docs.google.com/document/d/1OLQBLt6Jdxf-jwwL4fv-EbO7GBrEf3zZu0EmfQsfsP0/edit?hl=en_US or http://www.helium.com/items/263976-aspergers-syndrome-what-it-is. More information is available at his website: http://ahoorwitz.googlepages.com

Co-author **Andrea Sheerer** modeled an extreme range of facial expressions in this book in order to illustrate many different feelings. Andrea graduated at SUNY Plattsburgh with a B.A. in Art History and currently lives in the Adirondacks. She is a manager at a national bookstore where she is able to express her love of books by teaching children the joys of reading. Andrea also grew up with learning and comprehension disorders, and, as a result, has personal insight into the struggle of children's understanding during the challenges of learning throughout the stages of intellectual development.